HAL•LEONARD INSTRUMENTAL PLAY-ALONG

AUDIO ACCESS INCLUDED

PLAYBACK+
Pitch • Balance • Loop

ALTO SAX

Disney Aladdin

T0081423

Audio arrangements by Peter Deneff

To access audio visit:
www.halleonard.com/mylibrary
Enter Code
6119-8116-7307-8948

Motion Picture Artwork TM & Copyright © 2019 Disney

ISBN 978-1-5400-6236-9

HAL•LEONARD®

Visit Hal Leonard Online at
www.halleonard.com

Contact us:
Hal Leonard
7777 West Bluemound Road
Milwaukee, WI 53213
Email: info@halleonard.com

In Europe, contact:
Hal Leonard Europe Limited
42 Wigmore Street
Marylebone, London, W1U 2RN
Email: info@halleonardeurope.com

In Australia, contact:
Hal Leonard Australia Pty. Ltd.
4 Lentara Court
Cheltenham, Victoria, 3192 Australia
Email: info@halleonard.com.au

Contents

ARABIAN NIGHTS
(2019)

ALTO SAX

Music by ALAN MENKEN
Lyrics by HOWARD ASHMAN
BENJ PASEK and JUSTIN PAUL

ONE JUMP AHEAD

ALTO SAX

Music by ALAN MENKEN
Lyrics by TIM RICE

FRIEND LIKE ME

ALTO SAX

Music by ALAN MENKEN
Lyrics by HOWARD ASHMAN

PRINCE ALI

ALTO SAX

Music by ALAN MENKEN
Lyrics by HOWARD ASHMAN

SPEECHLESS

ALTO SAX

Music by ALAN MENKEN
Lyrics by BENJ PASEK
and JUSTIN PAUL

A WHOLE NEW WORLD

ALTO SAX

Music by ALAN MENKEN
Lyrics by TIM RICE